Fun Holiday Crafts
Kids Can Do

Halloween Crafts

Fay Robinson

E **Enslow Publishers, Inc.**

40 Industrial Road   PO Box 38
Box 398   Aldershot
Berkeley Heights, NJ 07922   Hants GU12 6BP
USA   UK

http://www.enslow.com

Library of Congress Cataloging-in-Publication Data

Robinson, Fay.
      Halloween crafts / Fay Robinson.
          v. cm. — (Fun holiday crafts kids can do)
      Contents: Hairy tarantula—Bat puppet—Haunted house—Ghoulish helping hand—Trick-or-treat coffin—Ghostly guest—Halloween pop-up card—Ghosts in the graveyard—Bats on a branch—Creepy Halloween necklace.
      ISBN 0-7660-2236-6 (hardcover)
      1. Halloween decorations—Juvenile literature. [1. Halloween decorations. 2. Handicraft.] I. Title. II. Series.
TT900.H32R63 2003
745.594'1646--dc21

                                        2003007220

Printed in the United States of America

10 9 8 7 6 5 4 3 2 1

To Our Readers: We have done our best to make sure all Internet addresses in this book were active and appropriate when we went to press. However, the author and the publisher have no control over and assume no liability for the material available on those Internet sites or on other Web sites they may link to. Any comments or suggestions can be sent by e-mail to comments@enslow.com or to the address on the back cover.

Illustration credits: Crafts prepared by Margaret Frase.
                                Photography by Carl Feryok.

Cover Photos: Carl Feryok

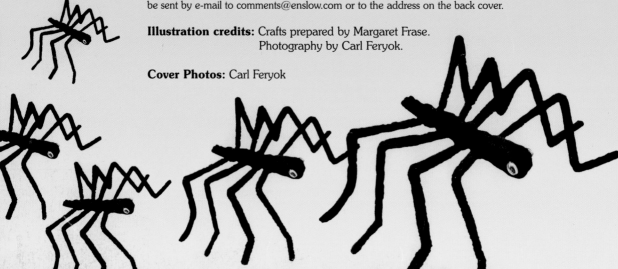

Contents

Safety Note: Be sure to ask for help from an adult, if
needed, to complete these crafts!

introduction

The fall wind blows. Leaves tumble from the trees. Kids in costumes are going from house to house. What is going on here? Why, it is Halloween, of course!

People called Celts (KELTZ) may have started this holiday long ago. In autumn, they celebrated the harvest. It was the end of the growing season. Winter would be coming soon.

Winter was a time of darkness and fear for the Celts. They believed that ghosts would come out on the night of their celebration. So, the Celts dressed in costumes so that the "evil spirits" would not know who they were.

All Souls' Day was also celebrated in the fall. This holiday honored the souls of the dead.

On this day, the poor went from door to door to beg for food. They may have been the first trick-or-treaters.

Later, these and other fall celebrations became one holiday: Halloween!

So, put some spiders around your house. Plant some ghosts in your garden. Use the crafts in this book to make your Halloween scarier (and more fun) than ever!

Hairy Tarantula

There is nothing like a hairy tarantula to make your home look creepy!

What You Will Need:

- 6 black pipe cleaners
- white glue
- wiggle eyes
- scissors
- string

1. To make the tarantula's body, use two pipe cleaners. Wrap them around the fingers of one hand.

2. Pull the pipe cleaners off and press them together, as shown.

3. To make the legs, fold another pipe cleaner in half. Put the center of the fold near one end of the body. Leave a space for the tarantula's head.

4. Wrap the pipe cleaner down under the body. Twist the ends back up. Cross them over the top. Repeat this with the three other pipe cleaners.

5. To make leg joints, fold each leg up, then down, then up again, as shown.

6. Glue a google eye to each side of the spider's head. Let the glue dry well.

7. Cut a piece of string and tie it to your tarantula. Hang the tarantula from a doorway or window.

Start with two pipe cleaners. . .

Wrap and press them together. . .

Fold a third pipe cleaner around the body. . .

Then, twist it around and bend the legs. . .

Tie a black string to it. . .

Add the eyes and your creepy, crawly spider is finished!

Holiday Hint:

To really scare your family, make a bunch of hairy tarantulas. Hang them all around your house!

Bat Puppet

Who knows more about the dark night than a bat? Let a bat puppet tell you its Halloween secrets.

What You Will Need:

- black and white felt (or construction paper)
- scissors
- white glue
- old black sock
- white yarn

1. Cut two circles from the white felt or construction paper. Cut two smaller circles from the black felt or construction paper. Use the patterns on page 26, if you like. These will be your bat's eyes.

2. Glue the black circles in the center of the white circles. When they are dry, glue the eyes near the toe end of the sock.

3. Cut a piece of yarn for the mouth. Glue it to the sock.

4. Cut two fangs from the white felt. Use the pattern on page 26, if you like. Glue them onto the mouth.

5. Use the pattern on page 26 to make ears from the black felt. Glue the ears to the top of the sock, as shown.

6. Use the pattern on page 26 to make two wings out of black felt. Glue them to the bat's back.

7. Let the glue dry well before using your bat puppet.

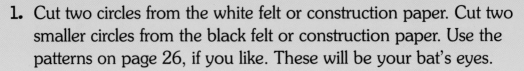

Start by making two eyes...

Glue them to the sock...

Add the scary fangs...

Your bat is ready for a ghoulish good time!

Holiday Hint:

Use your bat puppet to tell spooky stories to your friends. When you are not using the puppet, stuff another sock inside it. Then, hang the bat upside-down to sleep!

Haunted House

So your house is not haunted? You can make one that is!

What You Will Need:

- crayons or markers
- black, yellow, and orange construction paper
- scissors
- white glue
- spooky stickers (if you have them)

1. Use a white crayon to draw a haunted house or castle on black paper. If you like, you can use the pattern on page 27.

2. Draw large double doors in the middle. Draw some windows, as well.

3. Cut out your haunted house.

4. Cut around three sides of the doors. Do not cut the outside edges. Fold the doors open.

5. Cut around three sides of the windows. Do not cut the outside edges. Fold the windows open. If you like, you can cut yellow paper the same size and shape of the windows. Glue the yellow paper inside the windows to make it look like the lights are on inside the house.

6. Glue your haunted house to orange paper. Be careful not to glue your doors or windows shut!

7. Inside each window, draw a creepy creature—a skeleton, monster, or goblin. If you have stickers, you can use them, too. Finish your picture with a full moon and some spooky bats.

Draw your haunted house...

Carefully cut it out...

Cut out the windows and doors...

And no haunted house would be complete without eerie ghosts and goblins!

Holiday Hint:

Draw someone scary to greet the guests inside the door—maybe Frankenstein or Dracula!

Ghoulish Helping Hand

Need a hand on Halloween? Here is one!

What You Will Need:

- toilet tissue or cotton balls
- plastic or latex throwaway glove
- stapler
- green and black permanent markers
- green construction paper
- scissors
- black thread
- sheet of scrap paper
- craft stick
- white glue

1. Roll toilet tissue into small balls. Stuff them into the fingers and thumb of a plastic or latex glove. (You can use cotton balls instead, if you have them.) Fill the rest of the hand up to the wrist of the glove.

2. Staple the wrist shut.

3. Use the green marker to draw fingernails. Or, cut nail shapes from green construction paper and glue them to the tips of the fingers. Use the black marker to add wrinkles to make the hand look creepy.

4. To make your hand hairy, cut pieces of thread. Put them on a piece of scrap paper.

5. Use a craft stick to spread glue on the back of the hand. Roll the hand onto the threads to make it hairy. Let it dry well.

Stuff the glove with tissue or cotton balls. . .

Add the fingernails and creepy wrinkles. . .

Use thread for the hairy bits. . .

Your ghastly, ghoulish hand is ready to spook your friends and family!

Holiday Hint:

Make lots of hands. Put them around the house in places that will spook your family. Shut one in the refrigerator. Have one hanging out of a dresser drawer. Leave one on someone's pillow!

Trick or Treat Coffin

What better way to carry your treats than in a coffin? Your friends will be dying to see what is inside!

What You Will Need:

- shoebox with a lid
- hole punch
- scissors
- white glue
- liquid soap
- black tempera paint
- paintbrush
- heavy string
- marker
- white and green construction paper
- tissue paper

1. Take the lid off the shoebox. Use the hole punch to make two holes on each of the long sides, just below the top of the box.

2. Mix a few drops of liquid soap into the black tempera paint. (This will make the paint stick to the surface of the shoebox.) Paint the outside of the box and the lid. Let them dry.

3. Tie a piece of string through the holes to make a handle for your coffin. Make sure the string is long enough to let you open and close the coffin easily.

4. Use a marker and some white construction paper to decorate the lid of your coffin with the letters "R.I.P." (This means "Rest in Peace.") Use the pattern on page 28, if you like. Glue the white construction paper to the top of the shoebox. You can also glue "grass" made from green construction paper along the bottom of your coffin.

5. Line the inside of your coffin with tissue paper.

Paint a shoebox black and add holes for handles. . .

Knot strings to make handles and add "grass" to the bottom. . .

R.I.P.

R.I.P.

Decorate the lid. . .

Add candy and treats that even monsters can't resist!

Holiday Hint:

Take your coffin with you when you go trick-or-treating. Use it to hold your treats.

RIP
HERE LIES
the
GHOST
of
CASPER
1600-1700

Ghostly Guest

What would Halloween be without a ghost around the house?

What You Will Need:

- white balloon
- rubber bands or string
- washable markers
- old white sheet or pillowcase (be sure to ask for permission!)
- safety pin
- ribbon (optional)

1. Blow up the balloon. Knot the end or use a rubber band to close it tightly.

2. Use the washable markers to draw a ghostly face in the middle of the sheet or at the top of the pillowcase. Or, use the pattern on page 28.

3. Pin a piece of string to the top of the head with a safety pin.

4. To make your ghost's head, put the balloon in the middle of the sheet or inside the pillowcase. Pull the sheet around it. Tie it in place with a piece of string or use a rubber band. If you like, use ribbon to dress your ghost up with a bow tie to cover the rubber band or string.

Blow up a white balloon. . .

Draw the ghost's face. . .

Carefully pin the string to the top. . .

Add the bow tie. . .

Your ghost is ready to haunt your house on Halloween night!

Holiday Hint:

Hang your ghost in your bedroom doorway. It can greet (and scare) anyone who dares to come in! When Halloween is over, take your ghost apart. If you have used washable markers, the face should wash off.

17

Halloween Pop-Up Card

This card is sure to give someone a Halloween scare!

What You Will Need:

- construction paper in different colors
- scissors
- envelope
- markers
- white glue

1. Fold a sheet of paper in half to make the card. Trim the card so that it fits into your envelope.

2. With the markers, draw a spooky Halloween picture on the outside of the card.

3. Underneath the picture, write a Halloween greeting. Or, write the first part of a Halloween riddle, such as "What is a ghost's favorite color?" (The answer is in step 8.)

4. On another sheet of paper, draw a spooky Halloween ghost or creature. Cut it out. Use the markers to give it a scary face.

5. To make your ghost pop up, make a spring out of paper. Cut two strips of construction paper. Glue the ends together in an L-shape.

6. When the glue is dry, fold the top strip down over the other. Then fold the other strip back over the first, as shown. Keep doing this until you have folded all the paper.

7. Glue one end of the spring to the inside of your card. Glue the other end to your ghost or creature.

8. Write something on the inside of the card. If you wrote the first part of the riddle in step 3 on the outside, write "BOO" in large letters on the inside. (Get it?)

Fold a piece of paper in half and draw the front of your card...

Cut out a spooky ghost or creature...

Make an L-shape from two strips of paper glued together...

What is a ghost's favorite color?

Boo!

HAPPY HALLOWEEN!

Carefully fold them as shown to make the spring...

Glue the spooky ghost or creature onto the spring and your card is ready to surprise a friend!

Holiday Hint:

Put your card inside the envelope and mail it to a friend for a Halloween laugh!

Ghosts in the Graveyard

Turn your yard into a graveyard with these ghostly visitors!

What You Will Need:

- clean, dry white foam trays (from the grocery store)
- black permanent marker
- scissors
- craft sticks
- white glue

1. Draw one ghost shape on each foam tray with the markers. (Use the pattern on page 29 or make your own ghostly shapes.) Draw eyes and a frightful mouth on each ghost.

2. Cut out each ghostly shape.

3. Glue a craft stick to the back of each ghost.

Draw your spooky ghost on a foam tray. . .

Carefully cut it out. . .

Glue a stick to the back and your ghost is ready for some frightful fun!

Holiday Hint:

"Plant" your ghosts in your yard on Halloween. If you do not have a yard, you can plant your ghosts on your windowsills, in soda cans, or in other containers.

Bats on a Branch

Bats will fly through your bedroom on Halloween night!

What You Will Need:

- black construction paper
- white crayon
- scissors
- wiggle eyes
- white glue

- hole punch (optional)
- heavy string or black yarn
- 4 branches—one longer and thicker than the others

1. With a white crayon, draw five or six bats on black paper (or use the patterns on page 29).

2. Cut them out. Then, carefully draw the eyes with the white crayon or glue on wiggle eyes.

3. Punch a hole at the top of each bat with the hole punch and tie on different lengths of string or yarn. If you do not have a hole punch, you can glue the string or yarn to the back of each bat.

4. Tie one bat to each end of each branch.

5. Tie the branches together, as shown. Use the thickest, longest branch at the top. Tie the smaller branches to it. You have made a bat mobile!

Draw your bats on black paper. . .

Carefully cut them out. . .

Glue the string to the back and tie each one to a branch. . .

Your bats are ready to fly through the moonlit night!

Holiday Hint:

Hang the bat mobile from your bedroom doorframe or tape it to your ceiling. (Get an adult to help you) Open the windows or turn a fan on low and watch your bats fly!

23

Creepy Halloween Necklace

Wear a skull or shrunken-head monster necklace on Halloween to scare away ghosts and goblins!

What You Will Need:

- markers
- cardboard
- craft stick
- white glue

- scissors
- hole punch
- black yarn or string

1. With a marker, draw a small skull, monster, shrunken head, or other scary face on cardboard.

2. Draw eyes and teeth or other creepy features. Let the drawings dry for a minute.

3. Use the craft stick to spread a thick coat of white glue over the cardboard skull or head. Spread the glue past the edges. Let the glue dry.

4. When the glue has turned clear, cut out your cardboard head.

5. Make a hole in the top of it with the hole punch.

6. Cut a piece of yarn or string long enough to fit over your head. Pull the yarn or string through the hole in the top of your design. Tie the ends together in a knot.

Start by drawing a creepy monster...

Carefully cut it out and punch a hole in the top...

Add some yarn and your necklace is ready to wear!

Holiday Hint:

Make some creepy necklaces for your friends to get everyone in the mood for Halloween!

Patterns

Use tracing paper to copy the patterns on these pages. Ask an adult to help you cut and trace the shapes onto construction paper.

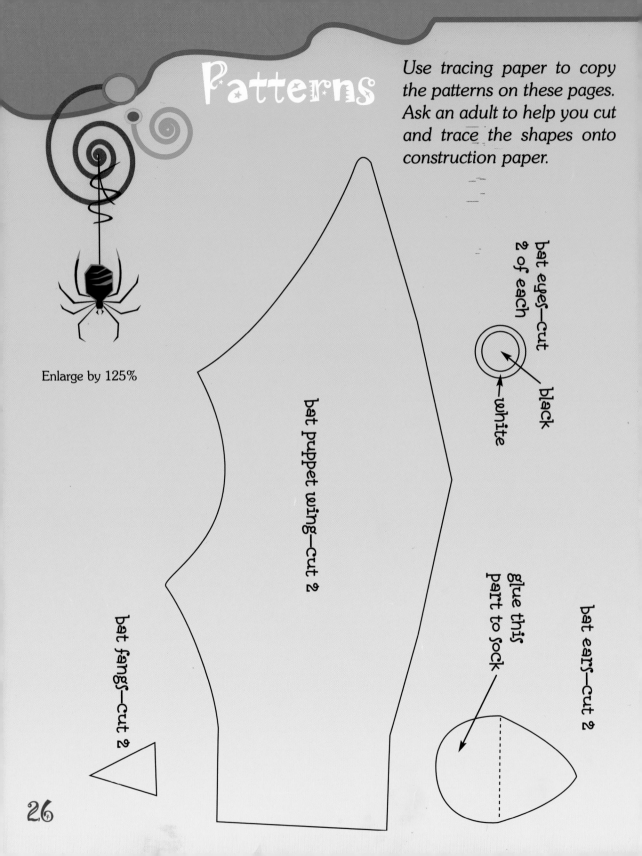

Enlarge by 125%

bat eyes—cut
2 of each

black

white

bat puppet wing—cut 2

bat ears—cut 2

glue this
part to sock

bat fangs—cut 2

26

Enlarge by 165%

27

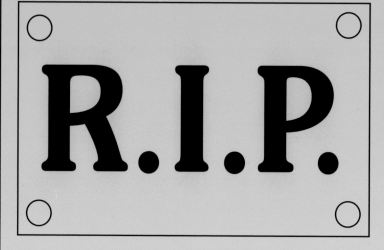

At 100%

Make sure the
ghost face is
about 6 inches
from the top of
the pillowcase.

At 100%

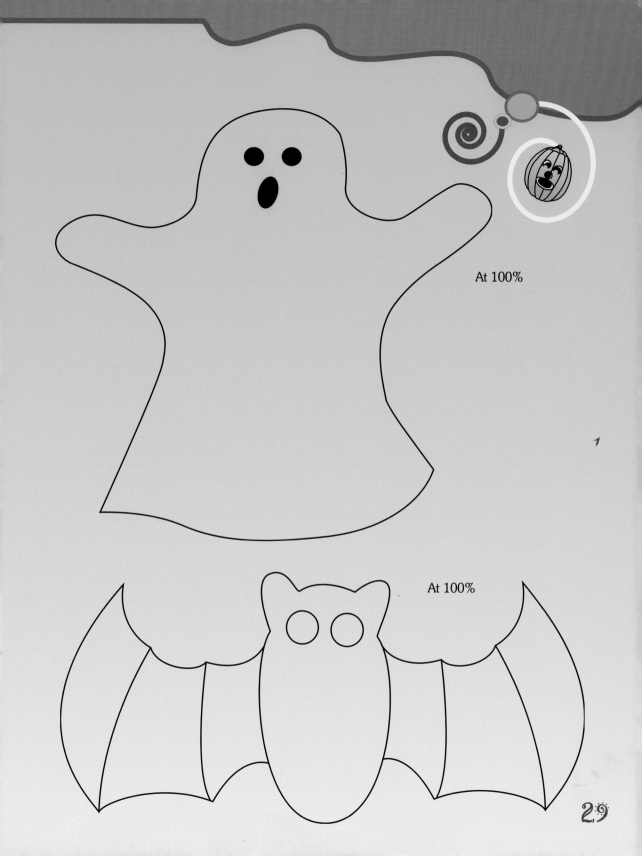

At 100%

At 100%

29

Reading About Halloween

Barth, Edna. *Witches, Pumpkins, and Grinning Ghosts: The Story of the Halloween Symbols*. New York: Turtleback Books, 2000.

Doring Kindersley Publishing Staff. *The Halloween Book: 50 Creepy Crafts for a Hair-Raising Halloween*. New York: Dorling Kindersley, 2000.

Horton, J. *Halloween Hoots and Howls*. New York: Henry Holt Books for Young Readers, 1999.

Kozielski, Dolores and Ferida Wolff. *Halloween Fun for Everyone*. New York: Turtleback Books, 1997.

Robinson, Fay. *Halloween—Costumes and Treats on All Hallows' Eve*. Berkeley Heights, N.J.: Enslow Publishers, Inc., 2001.

Roop, Peter and Connie Roop. *Let's Celebrate Halloween*. Brookfield, Conn.: Millbrook, 1997.

Internet Addresses

Halloween Magazine.com: The Official Halloween Safety Game

Halloween safety rules are included in this fun online game.

<http://www.halloweenmagazine.com/play2.html>

The History Channel: The History of Halloween

An interesting Web site about the origins, evolution, and traditions of Halloween.

<http://historychannel.com/cgi-bin/
frameit.cgi?p=http%3A//historychannel.com/
exhibits/Halloween/Hallowmas.html>

Index